The CAIRNGORMS of Scotland

Stuart Rae and Adam Watson

The CAIRNGORMS of Scotland

Stuart Rae and Adam Watson

Eagle Crag Ltd

Front cover	Crystals on rough granite boulders sparkle in June sunlight high in the Cairngorms
Back cover	Golden eagle - symbol of the wild
Half title	A delicate black darter basks on sun-warmed granite
Frontispiece	Dotterel - bird of the high plateau
Contents	A spring panorama from the Mounth massif, looking north to the Cairngorms

First published in 1998 by
EAGLE CRAG Ltd.
52 Osborne Place, Aberdeen, Scotland, UK. AB25 2DB

A catalogue record of this book is available from the British Library

ISBN 0 9533973 0 0

Origination and printing by J. Thomson Colour printers Ltd., Glasgow

Plateau and sky

A glorious September day on the arctic-like plateau, with autumn russet tints colouring the sparse wiry rushes

Winter on the high tops

Frozen fog - rime - clings to the summit tor on Beinn Mheadhoin

Foreword

This book is a tribute to the Cairngorms.

Both authors are north-east Scots. Stuart Rae took most of the photographs and Adam Watson gave most of the words. The photographs and captions are a personal selection from our own experience of the Cairngorms and their wildlife. All the photographs were taken during walks on the hill, as we believe the 'long walk-in' is the best way to appreciate the Cairngorms.

We have not used man-centred phrases such as 'dangerous' hills or 'fickle' weather. To us, the Cairngorms are not hostile. Rather, we experience humility towards them, have a deep respect for them, and feel at home there.

We are well aware of the qualities of local folk and their rich history and culture, of the climbing and other activities, and of the international conservation values. One of us is an author of books and other publications on these human aspects, and both of us work in the Cairngorms area and have written reports on its conservation. Here, however, we do not dwell on these subjects. In this book we have tried to express a relatively timeless view of nature in the Cairngorms.

In early work on the book we began with the convention of substantial text accompanied by photographs, but found this unbalanced and contrived. Instead we give simple captions to help explain what is illustrated and catch the imagination.

Let the photographs speak for themselves of the beauty, wonder and value of the Cairngorms.

Stuart Rae

Adam Watson

Morning clouds drift over an eastern plateau - Ben Avon

Roseroot

The flowers of this plant of the high cliffs provide rich nectar for butterflies and other insects, some of them visitors from the valleys far below

The Land

An Sticil - in Gaelic meaning *the kiln rafter*

Spindrift pours over and snow and ice plaster the 900-foot north wall of An Sticil - now usually called the Shelter Stone Crag - in the heart of the Cairngorms

A timeless scene - midsummer dawn

Far hilltops project like islands as a cloud inversion blankets the low strath of the River Dee. The sun rises above the tor of Clach Choutsaich - *Coutts' stone*.

The Cairngorms massif from the north

From the wide plain of Strath Spey, an impressive hill rampart rises above great tracts of woodland. A May snow shower highlights the Lairig Ghru pass, a former cattle drove route through the hills

Am Monadh Ruadh -
the red hill range

On long summer evenings, light softens the landscape. The red granite of the hills matches the warm-coloured bark of the Scots pines of Rothiemurchus, and brings to mind the old Gaelic name Am Monadh Ruadh. The hills of schist to the west of the River Spey are Am Monadh Liath - *the grey hill range*. Incomers coined the name 'Cairngorms' after the conspicuous hill Cairn Gorm (An Carn Gorm - *the blue hill*) which rises prominently on the Spey side of the massif. The expressive old name Am Monadh Ruadh is now seldom heard.

Gleann Dhe - glen of Dee (*Dee meaning river deity*)

The long Glen Dee with its steep rocky sides leads far up into the hills. Glacier ice shaped this land ten thousand years ago. Since the ice melted, the landscape has hardly changed, apart from the plants that now grow there.

Mist rolls in at late evening from the cool northern sea of the Moray Firth. The play of weather and light on the hills often changes by the minute.

Many miles of snowy domes under a midwinter sky - the Cairngorms from the south

A dotterel at home

The high plateaux of the Cairngorms are breeding grounds for many dotterel, which fly there from north Africa each spring. The mossy stony ground resembles other summer haunts of this colourful wader on the arctic tundras of Scandinavia and Russia.

The more rocky and snowy ground is the breeding haunt of the tiny snow bunting, whose song carries far across the highest tops and corries. Here the snow buntings are at the southern edge of their predominantly arctic breeding range which extends as far as the last land nearest to the North Pole.

The Cairngorms are a small extension of the arctic in Scotland.

A Cairngorms land-scape - hills clear for thirty miles, and immense sky and space

Water

Water drips into a bergschrund cave behind a snow cornice
that is detaching in summer heat from a clifftop

Subarctic desert

At 4000 ft on the plateau of Braeriach, wind-scoured gravel contrasts with fast-melting remnants of snow under a hot sun. Few plant species can endure such extreme conditions.

Brilliant green moss

A colourful sight in late summer and autumn is the rare apple-green moss *Pohlia wahlenbergii*, which carpets some spring heads at long-lying snowbeds

Easan De -
falls of Dee

The tallest high-altitude falls in the Cairngorms. The infant Dee, soon after rising at 4000ft on the plateau of Braeriach, emerges below a thick snow cornice to plunge down a dark wall of cliffs into the corrie below. The soft roar of Easan De echoes round the corrie, surging and fading as the wind eddies.

A high Lochan Uaine, ***green lochan***

The last snow and ice-flows float on the cold blue-green water of Lochan Uaine of Ben Macdui in June. An eagle's eye view looking down a thousand-foot cliff to boulder fields in the corrie far below.

A low Lochan Uaine, ***green lochan***

A soft breeze ripples the remarkably green water of An Lochan Uaine of Glen More, nestling below steep screes studded with old Scots pines

A sparkling silver thread tumbles into dark Loch Etchachan

Deep Loch Avon and its sandy beaches lie in a massive cliff-walled trough carved by glacier ice. The hillocky moraines beside the loch are striking evidence of the huge amounts of material moved here by glaciers ten thousand years ago. The long reddish gullies on the steep slopes mark the lines of water erosion after summer downpours.

Osprey, keen-eyed hunter of fish

Loch Garten of Spey

Soft reflections of pinewoods and hills on a warm summer dawn

Loch Kinord of Dee

A pale sun at midwinter noon sends gold light through wizened reed-heads and across thin ice

Loch Etchachan lies under deep snow and ice, below bulging snow wreaths that continue for a mile up to Ben Macdui

The foaming waterfalls, swirling pools and rocky walls of Ciste Dhe - *chest of Dee*

A fringe of birch, aspen and willow scrub survives on the steep banks, out of reach of hungry red deer

Uisge Dhe - ***water of Dee***

The middle reaches of Dee, shimmering over wide shingle beds, the summer home of oystercatchers and common sandpipers

Ice crystals above running water

Woodland

Deep in a natural woodland of the Cairngorms - dense patches of young pine and birch, open glades, older pines and birches, and stunted bogland trees at the loch edge

The Old Wood of Caledon

A complex array of old and young pines, birch and juniper, and aged dead limbs. Unlike a plantation, here is infinite variety.

A mantle of soft powder snow enhances the splendour and strength of a centuries-old Scots pine

A mild winter's day up the glen

Dark pines and banks of thawing snow form a black and white landscape, as veils of drizzle drift across the high hills

Every tree in the ancient pinewood is a unique individual

The intricate world on the floor of the old pinewood

Twisted caps of the false chanterelle sprout splendidly amidst blaeberry, feather-mosses, pine needles and cones

Blaeberry in autumn colour sets the woodland floor alight

Scottish crossbill

With its strong beak and crossed mandibles the Scottish crossbill can tear open the tightly-closed hard woody cones of Scots pines, to expose the soft nutritious seeds inside

Cock capercaillie

The biggest grouse in the world displays under old pines in spring

Birch twigs glisten after a winter rain shower

Junipers

In many places, juniper scrub extends beyond the woods on to the moor, and here the prickly leaves have protected a rowan sapling from grazing animals

Spring birch

The tender green of fresh leaves in May

Autumn birch

The rich gold of leaves in October

Roaring stag

During the rutting season, a big red deer stag mingles with hinds in their natural woodland home

Rowan roots

Thousands of rowan seeds disperse far and wide in the droppings of birds that have eaten the berries and then flown elsewhere. A few become trees. This one survived grazing animals by landing on the upturned root-plate of a wind-fallen Scots pine.

Aspen leaves and crisp autumn sky

The aspen's Latin name *Populus tremula* is particularly apt, for the leaves tremble even in the slightest wind

A dome of branches crowns a 'granny' Scots pine

Moor and Glen

Bod an Deamhain - *penis of the demon*, now usually called The Devil's Point, stands above Glen Dee

A thin partial covering of snow reveals subtle details in the land

Thousands of ice crystals on a peaty pool reflect oblique midwinter light

Glen Geusachan - *glen of little fir wood* - has been a treeless expanse of moorland for over two centuries

Woodland decline

The many pine and birch roots in the peat are relics of a former extensive woodland during a period of more continental climate over 3000 years ago

Peat has preserved this pine root for thousands of years

A mosaic of pools, boggy hollows and dry hillocks - a good breeding ground for greenshank

July

Bright yellow flowers of bog asphodel thrust into warm sunshine from cool wet sphagnum moss

Wader sentinel

A dunlin stands watchful atop a hummock on a moorland bog where its chicks hide until danger is past

The moor bursts into life

A myriad of heather flowers transforms entire hillsides in August, attracting innumerable insects, especially honey bees, and red grouse that feed on the flowers and shoots

On warm summer days, huge numbers of insects emerge simultaneously. Here a northern eggar moth dries its wings while hanging from a sedge before taking its first flight.

Moorland secret

A wigeon sits quietly on her eggs in a thick down-filled nest, hidden under a canopy of heather

A red deer calf's first day in the world

It lies sheltered and camouflaged amongst tall heather and blaeberry while its mother feeds on a distant hillside

Patience

A week-old mountain leveret waits perfectly still for its mother to return with a meal of rich warm milk once or twice a day

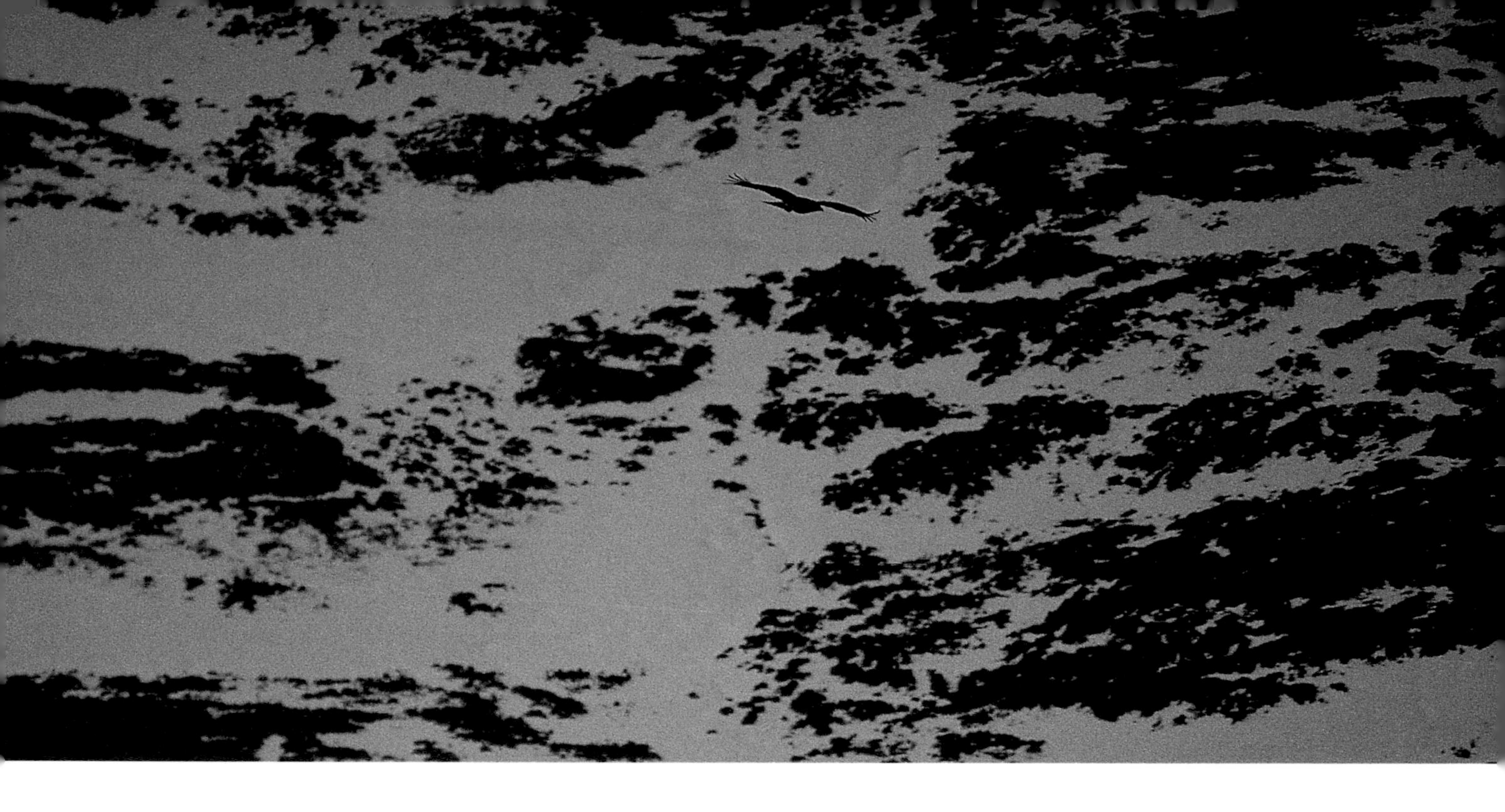

Winter hunter

A cock golden eagle on his hunting patrol is so inconspicuous against a contrasting patchwork of snow wreaths and dark heather that prey animals may well not notice him

Power

Golden eagles strike down their prey with the grip of their talons, and use their strong bills to tear off flesh

Heather flowers

High Ground

An Garbh Choire Mor - ***the great rough corrie***

The high Cairngorms in late winter, when blown snow has piled to great depths. These are the snowiest hills in Scotland, and this corrie holds Britain's most permanent snow, which has melted only thrice in over a hundred years, in 1933, 1959 and 1996.

A classic corrie - one of the finest in Scotland

The Northern Corrie of Lochnagar, the highest hill in the Mounth, with the snowy Cairngorms beyond. A long-past glacier gouged out this corrie, leaving imposing cliffs, bouldery slopes, and a deep hollow now filled by a dark lochan.

Sunlight catches a veil of summer sleet beyond Moine Mhor - *great peat-moss*, a rolling plateau of grassland and bog dotted with pools

West from the Cairngorms on a summer evening of heat haze, a succession of hills in silhouette stretches to the far horizon. On the right, the distinctive outline of Ben Nevis stands fifty miles away, near the West-Highland seaboard.

On Cairn Lochan, looking south-west to Cairn Toul

Acres of spiky rush tussocks among boulders and patches of granite grit roll on for miles

Imperceptible movement of an alpine plant

Many decades after starting life in the grit at the right, a crowberry plant has grown away from the prevailing wind into the lee of two boulders. It has put out new roots in its new sheltered site, and the old rootstock is now dead and detached from the ground. As lichens take many years to colonise bare alpine rock, the lichen-free zone on the adjacent rock shows where the crowberry foliage had once covered the rock.

In June, the prolific pink blooms of creeping azalea brighten windswept gravelly ridges on the high ground. This tiny azalea is one of the few plants that can thrive in such exposed, freely drained places.

Ptarmigan on nest

A hen ptarmigan, beautifully camouflaged and sitting absolutely still, incubates her six eggs. She has scraped her nest hollow into the thin cover of alpine heath beside a rock on the plateau.

A cock dotterel warms his three newly-hatched downy chicks

Autumn winds blow not only the light woolly seed-heads of the least willow, but also small stones

September frosts begin to colour sedges and rushes on the high plateau, across from Carn Etchachan

An arctic landform

In the arctic climate soon after the ice age, severe cold froze water deep into the soil. The physical forces exerted by freezing and thawing sorted and heaved large boulders and soil into a network of gelifluction lobes. Each lobe's lower part projects downhill in a lip of rocks, and the upper part contains soil with few rocks. Today, the vegetation reveals this difference, with heath on each freely-drained lip, and sedge and grass on the moister soil between the lips.

Winter on the way

A weak November sun fades before an advancing cloud mass bearing heavy snow.

Winter sun bask

A mountain hare has chosen to sit in the warmth of the late-afternoon sun while grooming its white winter coat

Ptarmigan in their element

On most winter days, powder snow drifts unceasingly over the windswept high ground

Subarctic landscape

- Coire Bhrochain of Braeriach

Midwinter sunset

The glens are already dark and only the hilltops are still bathed in the last fiery rays

Colour and Form

Crack lines on a north wall

A still moment

Evening view west to Cairn Toul (Carn an t-Sabhail - *hill of the barn*)

The great scree-swept trench of the Lairig Ghru divides the high Cairngorms

Snowy hill ridges

Low winter sun in late afternoon sets wind-blown snow alight

Crystals of frozen fog build up as feathery-like rime on summit rocks

Wind packs the snow and ice tightly on to the windward sides of the summits

Sharp dry frost grips smooth river-edge stones

A vertical granite face on the edge of the plateau

Rock lichens - tight and low on a plateau boulder

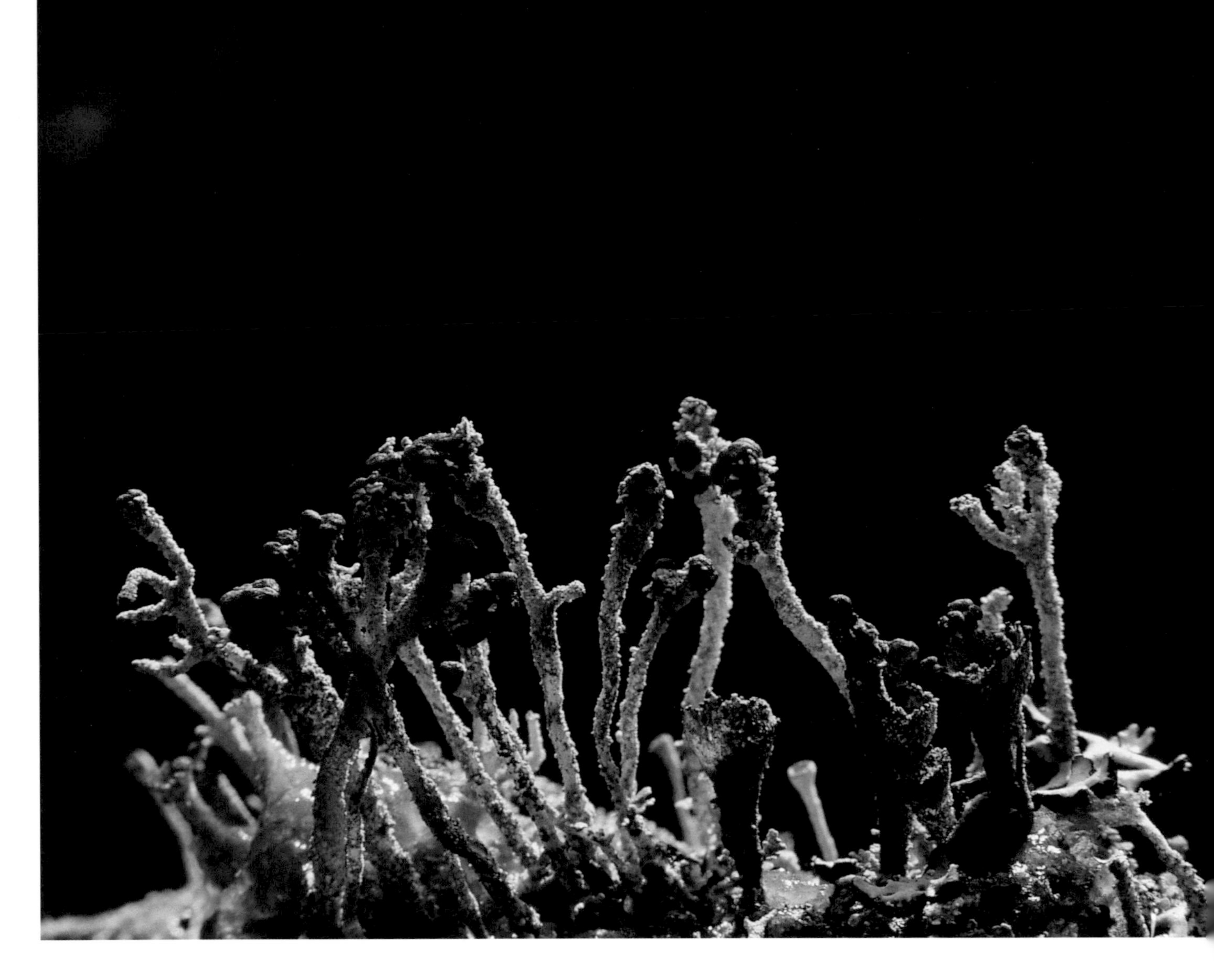

Ground lichens - stretching to the light in a woodland glade

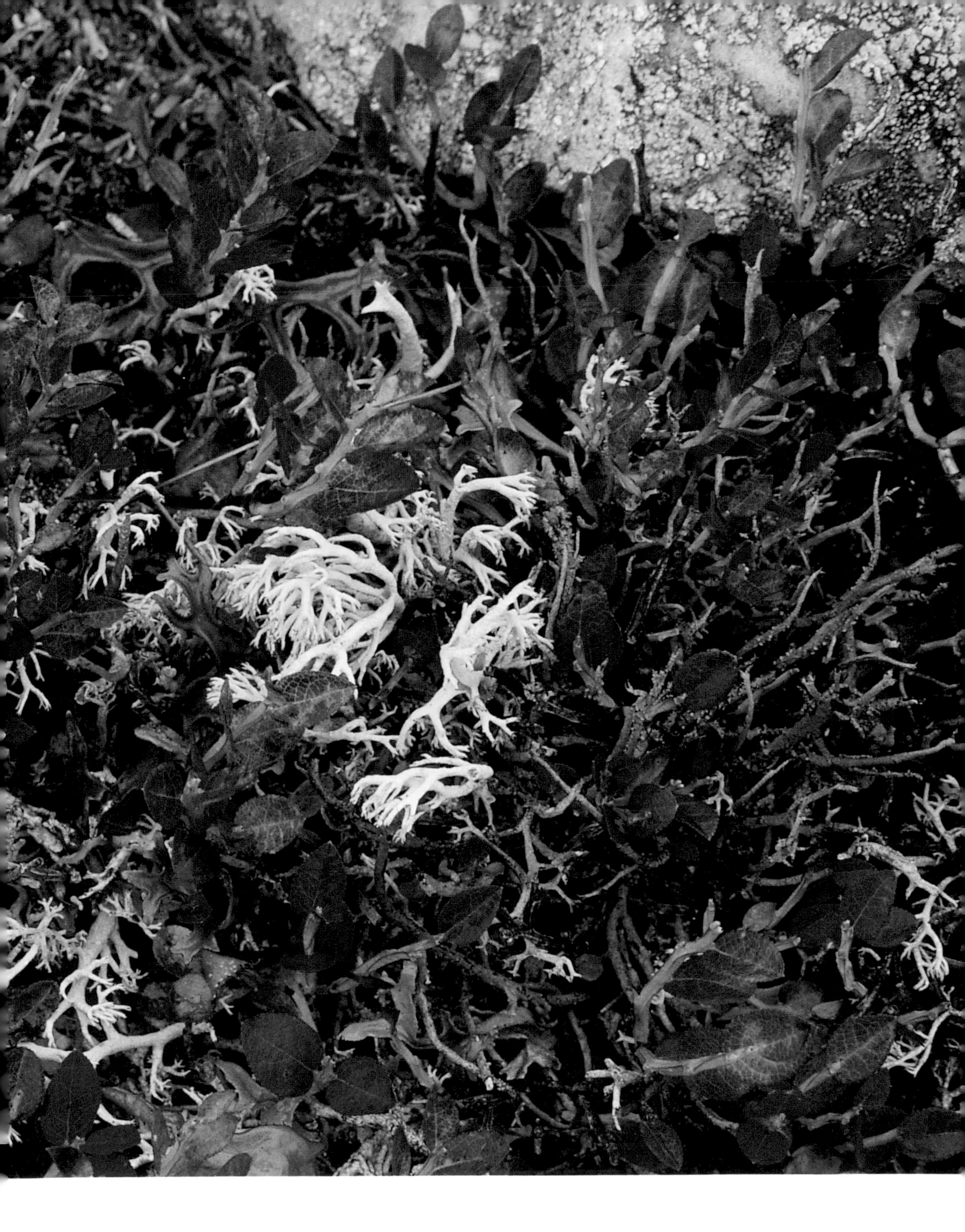

A natural tapestry of autumn blaeberry and lichens

High in a corrie, many mist droplets join up to become a water drop on each moss capsule.
The capsules contain reproductive spores.

Superb camouflage - a moth caterpillar feeding on heather (Beautiful Yellow Underwing)

Flat out

Prostrate heather in thin snow

The strength of spiral growth

The wood of a dead Scots pine whose bark has fallen off reveals its spiral growth that is less conspicuous in a living tree

Scots pine bark

A snow shower passes through lochside reeds

Ice-floes on a high lochan at midsummer

Clear water and clean sand - Loch Avon

Spring thaw

A stream, swollen with melted snow, spills over a corrie rim

Thunderstorm downpour

Peaty water surges into the glen after a torrential rainstorm

Rime and powder

Rime clings to boulders, soft powdery spindrift fills the cracks, and beyond rise distant snow-filled corries

A cock ptarmigan croaks loudly as he descends on a soaring song-flight, proclaiming his territory

The ptarmigan is the only bird hardy enough to be a resident of the high ground throughout the year. It is truly the bird of the high Cairngorms.

Moss gradually envelops the sun-bleached skull of a mountain hare. The natural cycle continues.

Selected further reading

Much has been much written about the Cairngorms. Some of the finest writings are in books now long out of print, although available from libraries or second-hand dealers. Modern information is more prolific, mostly in specialist scientific publications and climbing journals which readers can find in libraries. Below is a short list of books which give knowledgeable accounts of the Cairngorms and provide many references to other publications on the area.

Fyffe, A. & Nisbet, A. (1995). *The Cairngorms Rock & Ice Climbs, Vol 1 & 2.* Scottish Mountaineering Club Climber's Guide. Scottish Mountaineering Trust.

Gordon, S. (1925). *The Cairngorm Hills of Scotland.* Cassell, London.

MacConnell, J. & Conroy, J.W.H. (eds) (1996). *Environmental History of the Cairngorms.* Published as *Botanical Journal of Scotland* 48, No. 1. Edinburgh University Press, 22 George Square, Edinburgh, EH8 9LF.

Murray, I. (1992). *In the Shadow of Lochnagar*. I. Murray, Alt na craig, Ballater.

Nethersole-Thompson, D. & Watson, A. (1981). *The Cairngorms: their Natural History and Scenery.* Melven Press, Perth.

Watson, A. (1992). *The Cairngorms, Lochnagar and the Mounth.* Scottish Mountaineering Club District Guide. Scottish Mountaineering Trust.

Watson, A. & Allan, E. (1984). *The Place Names of Upper Deeside.* Aberdeen University Press, Aberdeen.

Stuart Rae has been going to the Cairngorms for thirty years, appreciating the wild landscape and the wildlife. He has spent much of his working life there, studying golden eagles, dotterel, ptarmigan, and plants. A freelance environmental consultant, writer and photographer, he has travelled to Scandinavia, Svalbard, the Alps, the Himalaya, and Australia. He now lives in Aberdeen, his home town, at the mouth of the River Dee.

Adam Watson has gone to the Cairngorms for sixty years. He has written books on the area's climbing, natural history, and place names, and many academic papers and articles on his scientific work there. These are mainly on wildlife, but also on snow patches and climate, soil erosion, human history and depopulation, and Gaelic dialect. He has worked in Iceland, Scandinavia, the Alps, Canada including Baffin Island, and the USA including Alaska. Born in Aberdeenshire, he now lives at Crathes by the River Dee.

Both authors are walkers, mountaineers, cross-country skiers, and biologists who studied ptarmigan for their PhD degrees.